matthew the Apostle

Banker and God's Storyteller

First Century

Lived in Galilee

**Feast Day: September 21
(November 16 in Eastern Churches)**

Community Role: Banker and Accountant

Text by Barbara Yoffie
Illustrated by Jeff Albrecht

Liguori

ONE LIGUORI DRIVE
LIGUORI MO 63057-9999

Dedication

To my family:
my parents Jim and Peg,
my husband Bill,
our son Sam and daughter-in-law Erin,
and our precious grandchildren
Ben, Lucas, and Andrew

To all the children I have had the privilege of
teaching throughout the years.

Imprimi Potest:
Stephen T. Rehrauer, CSsR, Provincial
Denver Province, the Redemptorists

Published by Liguori Publications
Liguori, Missouri 63057

To order, visit Liguori.org or call 800-325-9521.

p ISBN 978-0-7648-2555-2
e ISBN 978-0-7648-7006-4

Liguori Publications, a nonprofit corporation, is an apostolate of the
Redemptorists. To learn more about the Redemptorists, visit Redemptorists.com.

Printed in the United States of America
19 18 17 16 15 / 5 4 3 2 1
First Edition

Dear Parents and Teachers:

Saints and Me! is a series of children's books about saints, with six books in each set. The first set, *Saints of North America*, honors holy men and women who blessed and served the land we call home. The second set, *Saints of Christmas*, includes heavenly heroes who inspire us through Advent and Christmas and teach us to love the Infant Jesus. The third set, *Saints for Families*, introduces saints who modeled God's love within and for the domestic Church.

Saints for Communities explores six individuals from different times and places who served Jesus through their various roles and professions. Saint John Baptist de la Salle taught children and founded a familiar educational system. Saint Joan of Arc helped to bring peace to the country of France. The Apostle Matthew was a tax collector before deciding to follow Jesus. The Apostle Thomas preached and built churches. Saint Cecilia sang hymns to Jesus in her heart. And Michael the Archangel is well-known for his protection.

Which saint doubted Jesus' resurrection? Which one fought a heavenly battle? Which saint heard heavenly voices? Who sold everything he owned? Which saint was first named Levi? Which saint was married against her will? Find out in the *Saints for Communities* set—part of the *Saints and Me!* series—and help your child connect to the lives of the saints.

Introduce your children or students to the *Saints and Me!* series as they:

- **READ** about the lives of the saints and are inspired by their stories.
- **PRAY** to the saints for their intercession.
- **CELEBRATE** the saints and relate them to their lives.

saints of communities

 John Baptist
Teacher

 Joan of Arc
Soldier

 Matthew
Banker

 Thomas
Construction worker

 Cecilia
Musician

 Michael
Police officer

Jesus traveled from town to town and taught people about God's love. He healed the sick and helped the poor. Many people followed Jesus. They were called his disciples. Jesus chose twelve special men, called apostles, to preach his Good News to all nations. This is a story about the Apostle Matthew.

Matthew was a tax collector. He collected money from the people and gave it to the Roman government. In those days, most tax collectors were unfair and kept money for themselves. The people did not like how they were treated, and they probably did not like Matthew, either.

One day, Matthew sat at a table counting money. He saw a group of men on the road. Then he saw Jesus talking to some of his close friends. Jesus walked toward Matthew and said, "Follow me."

Matthew jumped up from the table. Coins fell to the ground. He left the bags of money and ran to Jesus. When Matthew reached Jesus, they both smiled. "Come to my house tonight," Matthew said. "We will eat dinner together. Bring all of your friends." Matthew invited his tax-collector friends. He wanted them to meet Jesus.

The guests shared a meal of fish, bread, and fruit. Everyone had a good time. Later someone asked, "Why does Jesus eat with tax collectors? They are sinners." Jesus replied, "Anyone can follow me." That day Matthew gave up his money and power and became a follower of Jesus'.

Matthew really liked Jesus and his friends. Many of the apostles traveled together. Every day they listened to Jesus teach. They saw him heal the sick and feed the hungry. Jesus said and did amazing things. He even performed miracles!

But some people did not like Jesus. His enemies put him to death on a cross. Matthew and the other apostles were very sad when Jesus died. Three days later, Jesus came out of the tomb. Jesus had risen from the dead!

The risen Jesus told his apostles, "I want you to go to towns near and far and teach people about me. I must return to my Father, but do not worry. I will send the Holy Spirit to help you." Jesus said goodbye and left for heaven.

One morning while the apostles were praying together, a strange thing happened. They felt the wind blow, and small flames appeared over their heads. They were filled with wisdom and courage. What could this be? "Jesus has sent us the Holy Spirit. We must tell everyone the Good News," they said.

The apostles traveled far and wide to teach and preach like Jesus. Matthew visited many towns and preached for years: "Let me tell you about a man named Jesus. He died for us, but he rose and lives forever! He is God's Son, our promised Savior." Many people listened to Matthew and believed.

Years later, Matthew wrote about Jesus. His stories told of Jesus' great love for all people. Matthew passed on what Jesus said, did, and taught. Today we read and hear these words in the Bible. We call his writings "the Gospel of Saint Matthew."

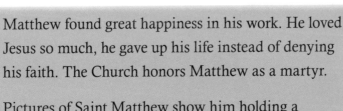

Matthew found great happiness in his work. He loved Jesus so much, he gave up his life instead of denying his faith. The Church honors Matthew as a martyr.

Pictures of Saint Matthew show him holding a pen or standing next to an angel. Angels are God's messengers and so is Saint Matthew. He is the patron of tax collectors, accountants, and bankers.

Think about what you would do.
Would you follow Jesus, too?

Dear God.

I love you.

Saint Matthew left his
old life to follow you.

He shared your words
and spread your truth.

Help me to follow you
more closely
and share your love
with others.

Amen.

NEW WORDS (Glossary)

Angel: A spiritual being, a messenger of God

Apostle: One of the twelve special men chosen by Jesus to preach the Gospel

Disciple: A person who follows the teachings of Jesus

Good News: The saving acts and words of God. Jesus died and rose again to give us forgiveness and eternal life

Gospel: Means "good news." The four books of the Bible, called Gospels, tell the life stories, teachings, and miracles of Jesus

Martyr: Someone who gives up his or her life on behalf of a belief or cause

Miracle: An amazing event that cannot be explained

Savior: The one who protects us from the dangers of evil and punishment for sin: Jesus Christ

In the Gospels of Mark and Luke, Matthew is called "Levi." Levi may have been his original name, and he took, or was given, the name Matthew when he became an apostle of Jesus'.